US GOVERNMENT ECONOMICS

Local, State and Federal

How Taxes and Government Spending Work
4th Grade Social Studies

Speedy Publishing LLC

40 E. Main St. #1156

Newark, DE 19711

www.speedypublishing.com

Copyright 2018

In this book, we're going to talk about how taxes and government spending work. So, let's get right to it!

TAX

TAXES
%
20%
40%
80%
100%
60%
JAN FEB MAR APR MAY JUN JUL AUG SEP OCT NOV DEC

In order for the United States government to pay for public services for its citizens as well as the salaries for government workers, there must be appropriate amounts of money allocated. This money comes from many different forms of taxation. Taxes that are paid to the federal government pay for the president's salary. Federal taxes also pay for the salaries of members of Congress and fund the military to protect the country.

S tate taxes fund the infrastructure of the state like roads and bridges. The state governor's salary is also paid by state taxes. At the local level, taxes collected by county governments and city governments help to fund schools and protection services, such as fire and police departments.

There are so many salaries and services that the United States government pays for that without money collected from taxes, the government wouldn't be able to run.

FEDERAL

TAXES

WHAT ARE TAXES?

Taxes are fees that the government at different levels places on the cost of goods, property or income. Taxes can be requested at the city, county, state or federal level. For example, your state probably charges a sales tax on many different items that you buy at the store. Sometimes there is a "luxury tax" on items that people want, but don't really need.

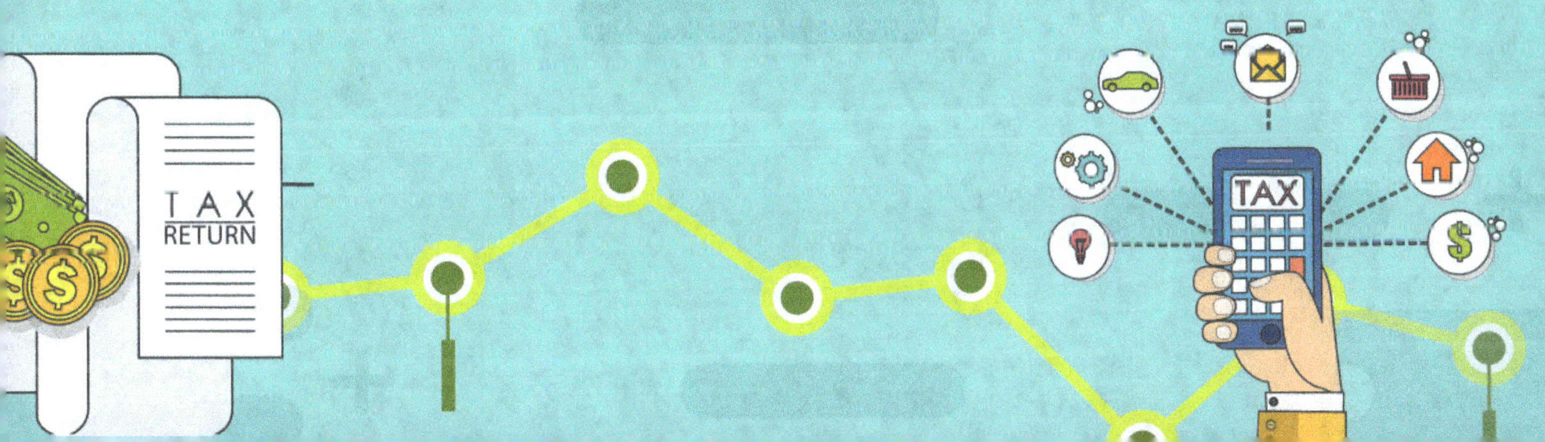

M
M+
+
=
INCOM
A

E TAX
CT
Another type of tax is a tax on income that people earn from working for someone else or from working on their own businesses. If your parents work for an employer, then they have taxes removed from their paycheck every time they get paid.

On tax day, which is April 15th, if they haven't paid enough in tax, then they will have to remit an additional payment with their tax return. Sometimes, if they have overpaid, they'll receive money back from the Internal Revenue Service, called the IRS for short.

eople who are self-employed and own their own businesses pay tax on their income and they also pay an additional "self-employment tax." Most states collect taxes on income as well.

DID AMERICANS ALWAYS PAY TAXES ON INCOME?

United States citizens didn't always pay an income tax. For the first 130 years that the United States was an independent nation, no taxes were levied on income.

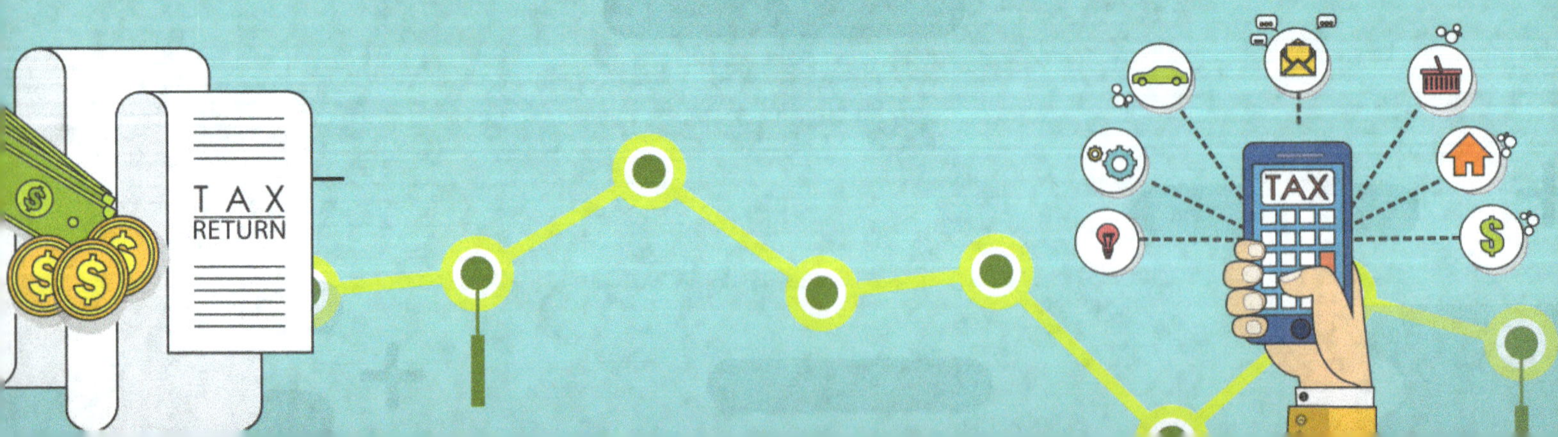

BILL
TAX
$

Part of the reason for this was because Great Britain had over-taxed the colonies and this was one of the major causes of the American Revolutionary War.

However, in the year 1913, when Woodrow Wilson was President, the 16th Amendment was passed. This Amendment gives the power to the Federal government to collect tax on income.

WHY DO WE NEED TAXES?

Taxes help the government pay for services that citizens need. The federal taxes that are collected are allocated for many different programs. Here is a breakdown of how the United States government allocates the federal taxes it collects.

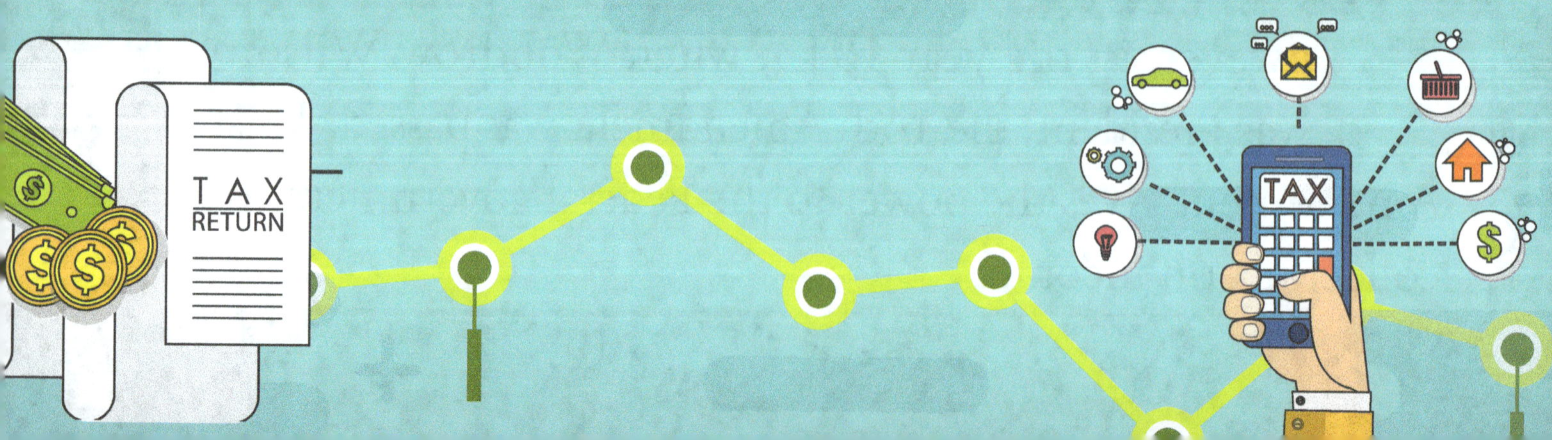

Social Security for the elderly, 24%

- Medicare for the elderly, 15%
- Defense and military programs to protect the United States, 15%

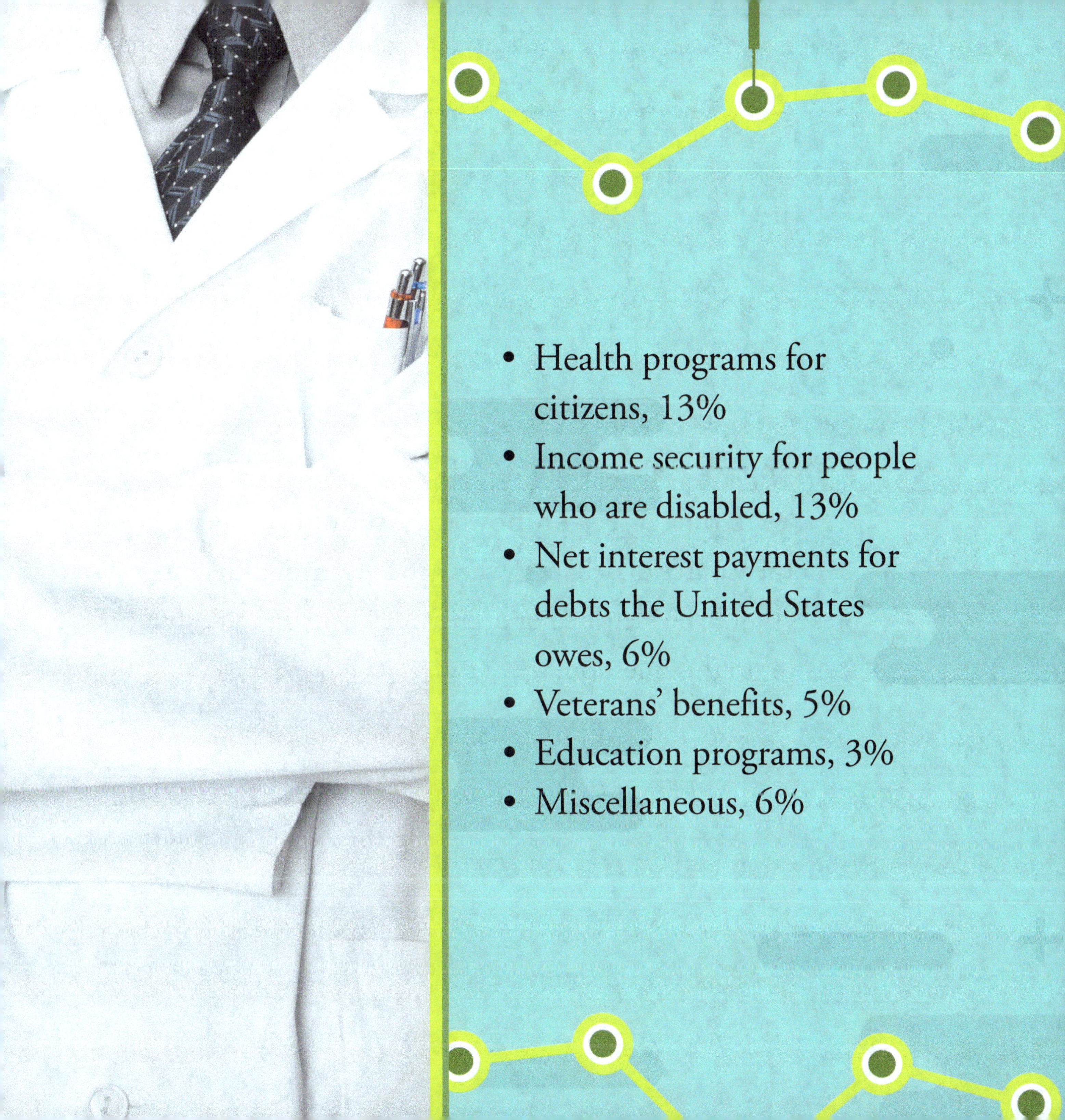

Health programs for citizens, 13%
Income security for people who are disabled, 13%
Net interest payments for debts the United States owes, 6%
Veterans' benefits, 5%
Education programs, 3%
Miscellaneous, 6%

People are always talking about taxes because not everyone agrees on how they should be spent. Another source of debate is whether the rate of different taxes should be increased or decreased. There isn't an easy answer to this question.

If the government doesn't charge any taxes, then there wouldn't be any money to run the needed programs. If it takes all of the money that its citizens earn, then no one would want to work anymore.

Many people feel that the lower and middle classes pay too much in tax and the wealthy don't pay enough in tax.

WHAT ARE THE DIFFERENT TYPES OF TAXES?

There are many different types of taxes that individuals and businesses pay. Here are a few of the most important ones.

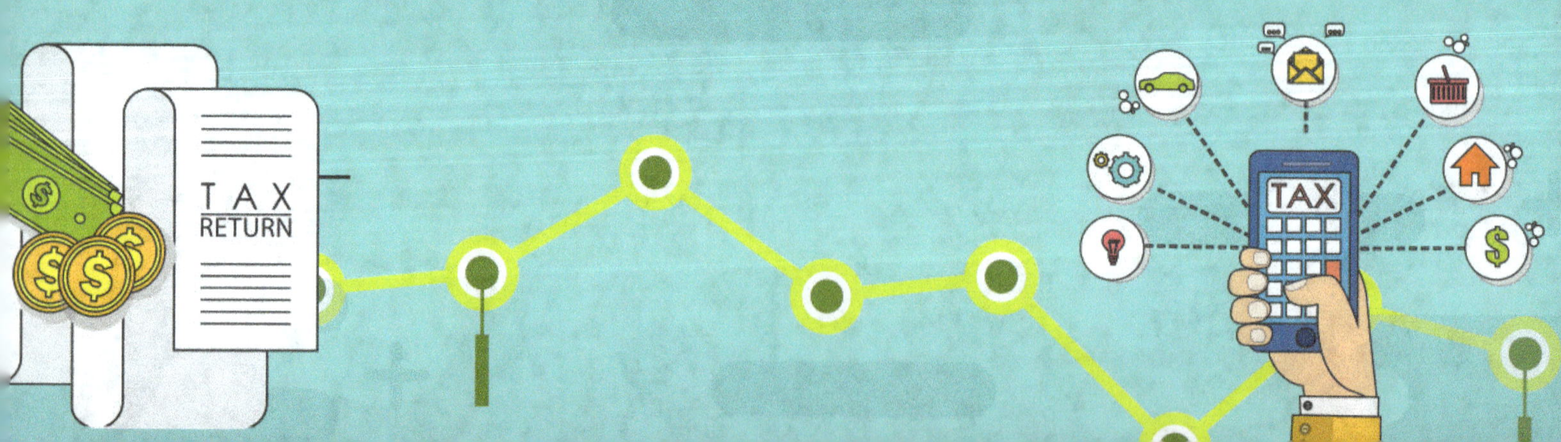

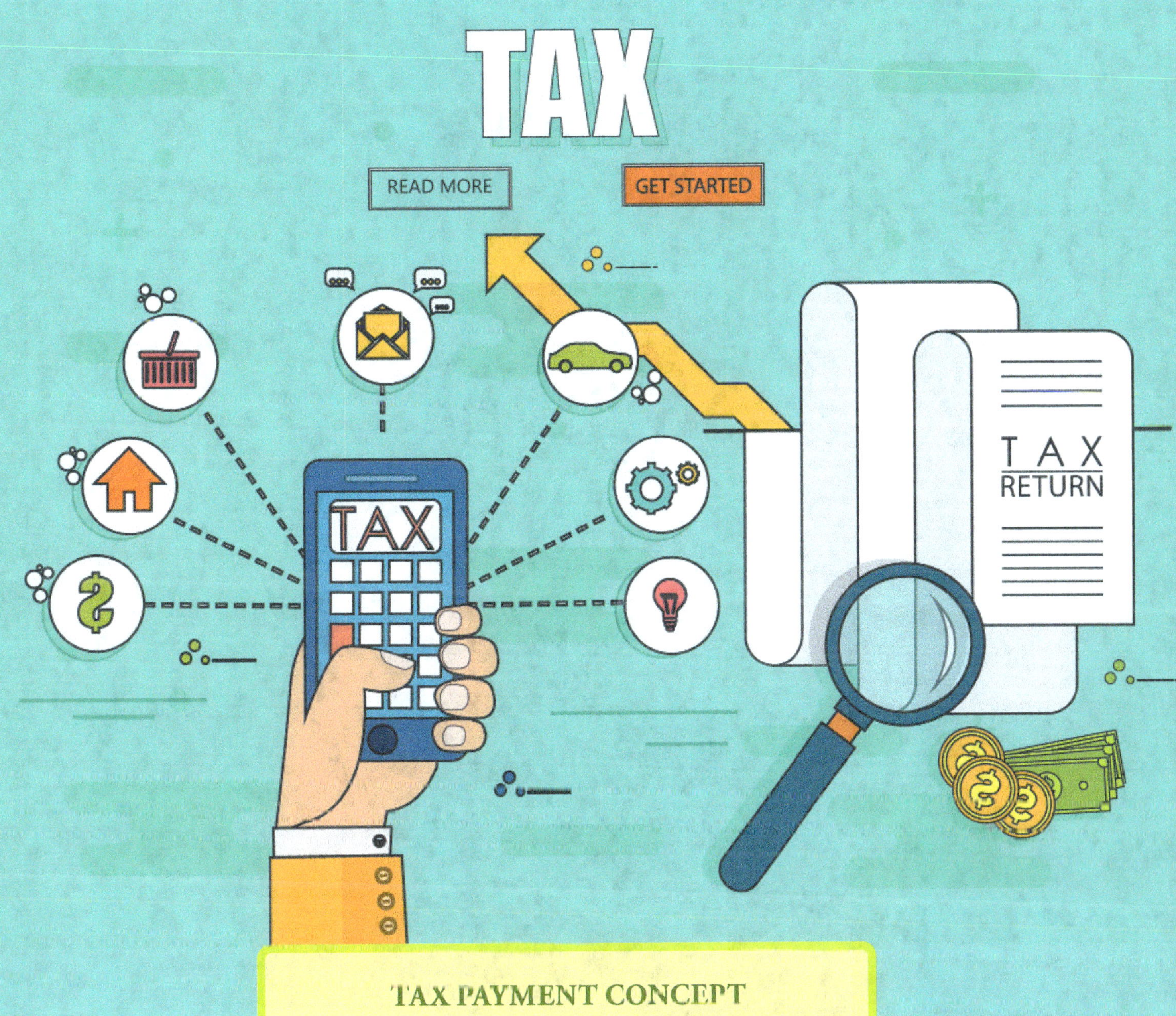

TAX
READ MORE
GET STARTED
TAX
TAX
RETURN
TAX PAYMENT CONCEPT

SALE TAX

SALES TAX

If you buy anything at the store, in most states there is a sales tax added. Depending on the state you live in, some items aren't taxed and others are. For example, some states charge sales tax on food and others don't. The amount of the sales tax varies depending on where you live.

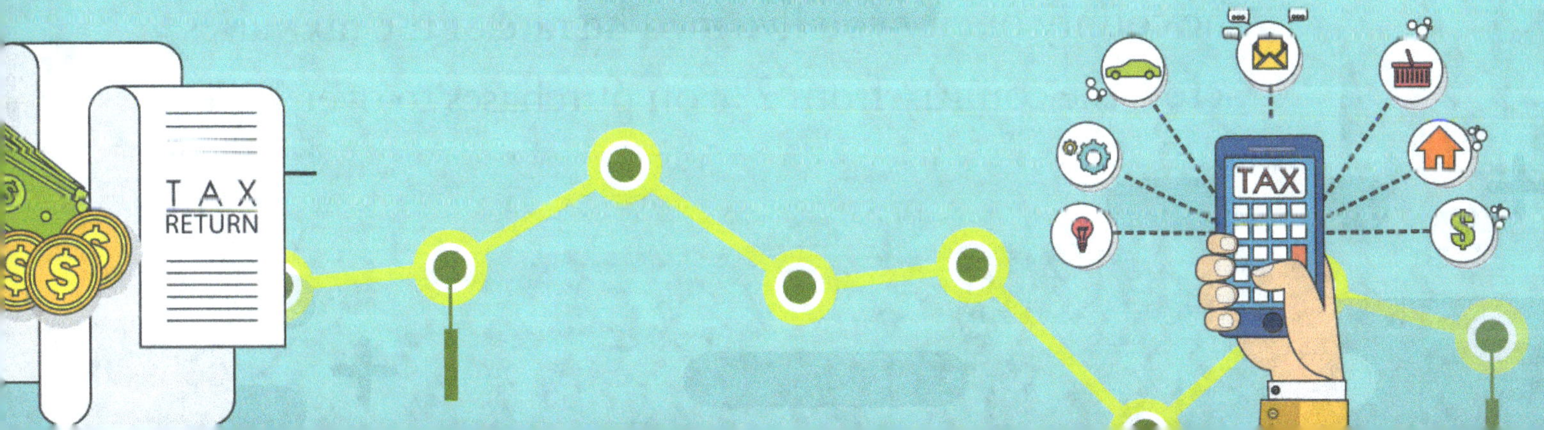

The sales tax charged may be a combination of the state's sales tax plus additional local taxes from the county or city you live in. The rate of the tax varies across the country from 2% on purchases to over 10%.

S TAX

Certain types of services are also taxed. For example, suppose you go to a local printer to get some flyers printed for an event. More than likely you will pay sales tax on the service of having the flyers printed. However, if you are a business owner and you are buying printing services for some books you are going to resell to another customer, then instead of paying the sales tax, you will collect the sales tax from the customer who buys from you.

Then, you will report the sales tax you collected from your customers and pay it to the state every quarter. In order to handle the transaction this way, you would need a resale permit.

CONTRACT
A SALES CONTRACT WILL LIST THE TAX THAT WILL
BE COLLECTED WHEN THE SALE IS COMPLETED

Taxes are complicated and sales tax is actually one of the easiest taxes to understand because as a consumer you will see the sales tax you have been charged on your receipts.

You'll be able to figure out what the percentage is. In fact, on big-ticket purchases, such as cars or boats, some people buy out of state so that they can save on the sales tax.

PROPERTY TAX

If your parents own a house or other real estate, then they pay taxes on their property. The amount of tax owed on the property will depend on the city and county where the property is located.

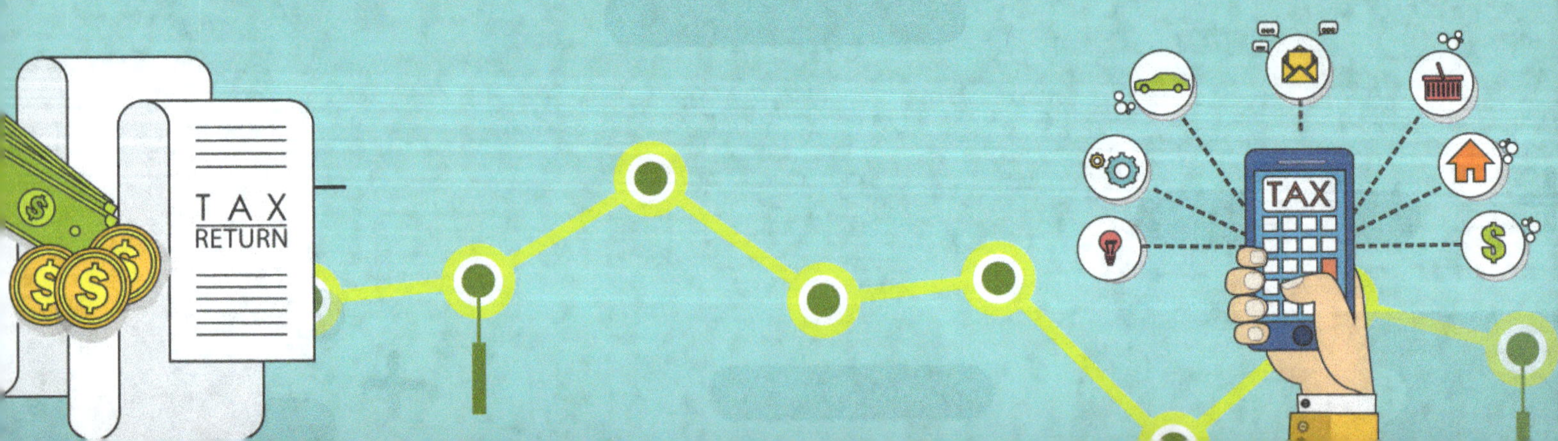

PROPERTY
TAXATION

It will also depend on the value of the property. For example, if the property is valued at $250,000 and the annual tax is 2%, then the property tax each year will be $5,000.

INCOME TAX

Most of the money that the federal government collects from taxes is from taxes on income that people make. The tax on income isn't a straight percentage calculation like sales tax or property tax.

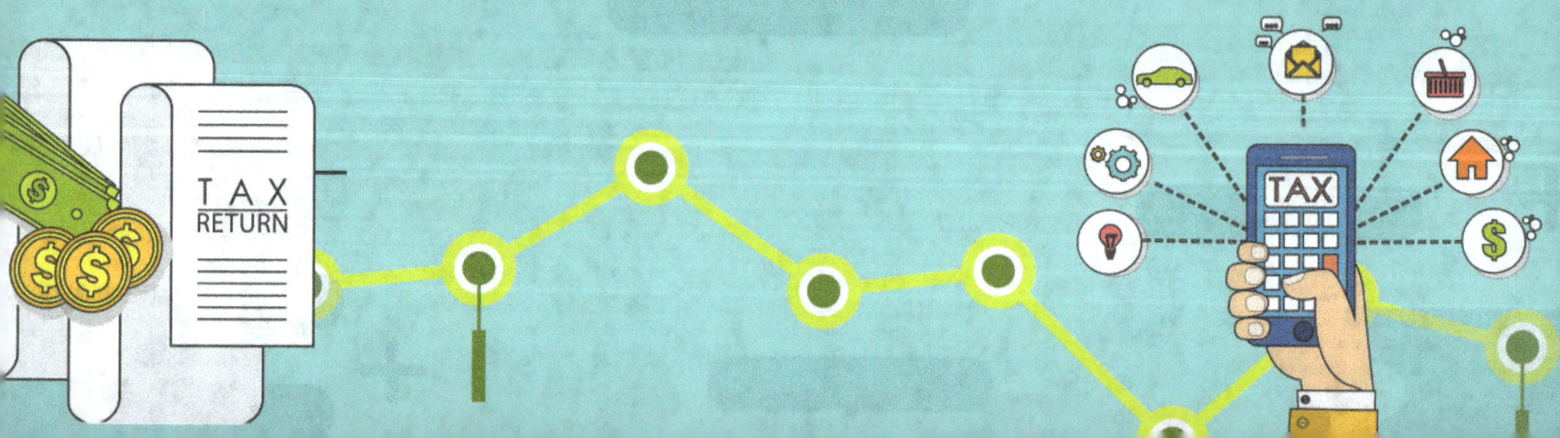

income
tax

The amount of income that is used for the tax calculation depends on your expenses and tax deductions. For example, if you own a home, the interest on the mortgage payment that you make is deducted from your taxes.

Some people have tax returns that are very simple to do and they do their own returns. Others have tax returns that are so complicated that without an accountant, they wouldn't be able to file their taxes.

The current document that fully explains the United States tax code is about 4 million words! Even some certified public accountants that are experts at preparing tax returns have trouble remembering all of it.

Form **1040**

Department of the Treasury—Internal Revenue Service

U.S. Individual Income Tax Return

(99)

For the year Jan. 1–Dec. 31, 2012, or other tax

Your first name and initial

Last na

beginning

If a joint

SOCIAL SECURITY

VALID FOR WORK

WITH INS A

Amount from line 37 (adjusted

Check
if.

You

Form 1040 (2012)

38

Tax and
Credits

39a

b

40

41

Standard
Deduction

Itemizes on a sep

deductions (fro

Subtract line 40 from

Exemptions.

Taxable

If your

You w

SOCIAL SECURITY TAX

In addition to the income tax that gradually comes out of your paycheck throughout the year if you are an employee, another tax that the government takes is for Social Security. You are actually paying yourself in advance for when you will retire in your sixties or seventies.

If you work for an employer, the employer must pay a percentage of this tax. The calculation is 6.2% for the employee and the same percentage for the employer. However, if you work for yourself, you must pay for both, which is a total of 12.4%.

MEDICARE TAX

Medicare is a health program for seniors. Once again, as you earn money, the government collects this tax so, when you retire, you'll have most of your health care paid for you. The rates for the Medicare tax are 1.45% if you work for a company as an employee. For those people who make a substantial income, sometimes the rate is 2.35%.

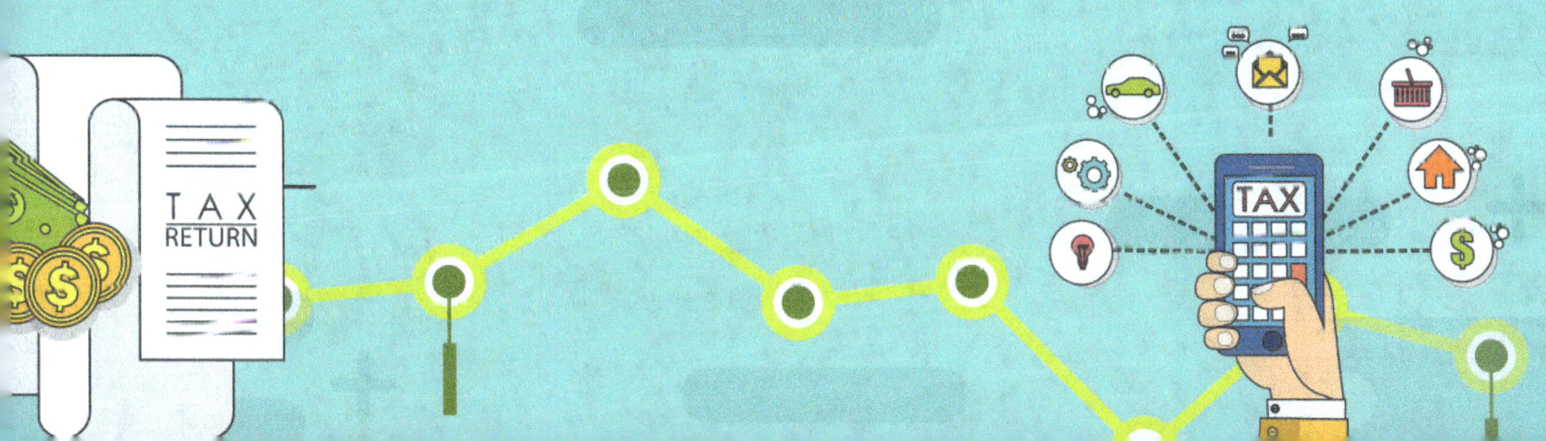

CORPORATE TAXES

Corporations and businesses pay taxes based on the profits they make in a given year. As with income tax, the computation of these taxes is complicated since there are also many different types of deductions that corporations and businesses can take.

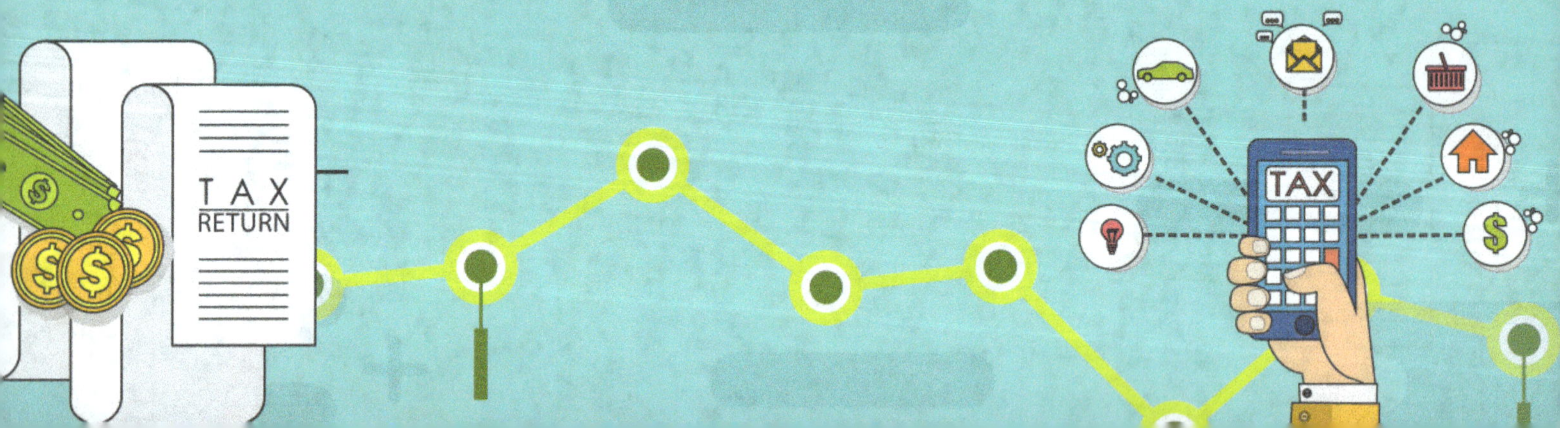

CORPORATE TAX
SALES
INVESTMENT
PROFIT
RISK
BUSINESS
LOAN
Series1
140
120
100
80
60
40
20
0
JAN FEB MAR APR MAY
90
80
70
60
50
40
30
20
10
0
Series1
NOV
SEP
JUL
MAY
MAR
JAN
20
40

Your Federal
Income Tax
For Individuals
TAX GUI
201
FOR IN
Get forms
AX

HOW MUCH DOES THE FEDERAL GOVERNMENT COLLECT IN TAXES?

In 2016, the United States government collected about $3.3 trillion, but almost $3.9 trillion was spent, so this means that the government is going into further debt.

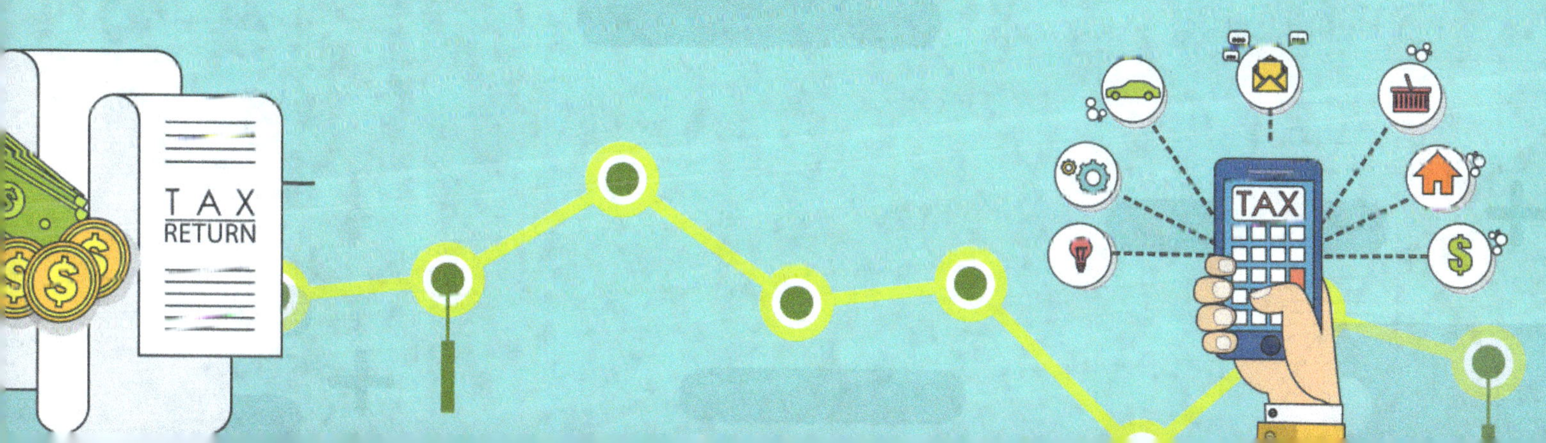

SUMMARY

The United States government needs money to run the different programs and services it provides for its citizens. The money comes from the different taxes that the government collects at the federal, state and local level. Politicians are always debating whether taxes should be increased or decreased.

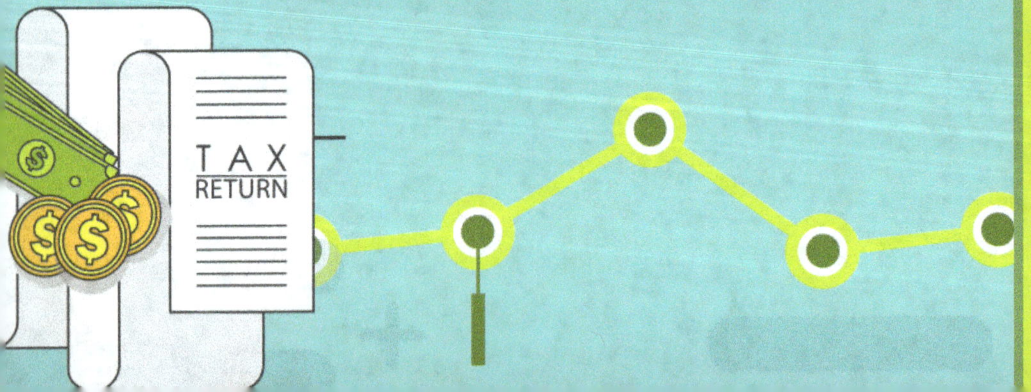

TREASURY BUILDING, WASHINGTON

DAY
TAX

Awesome! Now that you've read about how taxes and government spending work in the United States, you may want to read about the United States economy in the Baby Professor book Economics for Kids - Understanding the Basics of An Economy | Economics 101 for Children | 3rd Grade Social Studies.

Visit

BABY PROFESSOR
EDUCATION KIDS

www.BabyProfessorBooks.com
to download Free Baby Professor eBooks
and view our catalog of new and exciting
Children's Books